Western Attitudes
toward DEATH

THE JOHNS HOPKINS SYMPOSIA
IN COMPARATIVE HISTORY

The Johns Hopkins Symposia in Comparative History are occasional volumes sponsored by the Department of History at The Johns Hopkins University and The Johns Hopkins University Press. Each considers, from a comparative perspective, an important topic of current historical interest and comprises original essays by leading scholars in the United States and other countries. The present volume is the fourth. Its preparation has been assisted by the James S. Schouler Lecture Fund and the Phillip W. Haberman, Jr., Foundation.

Grand portal ("The Last Judgment") of the Cathedral of St. Etienne, Bourges. Photo Lauros-Giraudon.

Western Attitudes toward DEATH: From the Middle Ages to the Present

by PHILIPPE ARIÈS

translated by PATRICIA M. RANUM

THE JOHNS HOPKINS UNIVERSITY PRESS
Baltimore and London

The Johns Hopkins University Press, Baltimore, Maryland 21218
The Johns Hopkins University Press Ltd., London

Library of Congress Catalog Card Number 73-19340
ISBN 0-8018-1566-5

Library of Congress Cataloging in Publication data
will be found on the last printed page of this book.

Contents

Preface

In response to the invitation of the History Department of the Johns Hopkins University to lecture on the subject of history, political culture, and national consciousness, the author of *Le Temps de l'Histoire* and *Centuries of Childhood* replied that his interests had shifted considerably from the time when he had written those books. Philippe Ariès continued by saying that he had been working on a history of changing attitudes toward death in Western societies since the Middle Ages.

With fears about a language barrier dispelled by the assurance that there would be translations of his lectures, and with the support of the Schouler funds and the Phillip W. Haberman, Jr., Foundation, it became possible to invite Philippe Ariès to Hopkins to present the lectures which constitute this volume.

Convinced by his research that it was indeed the culture of the United States which has played the primordial role in changing Western attitudes toward death in the twentieth century, Ariès welcomed the opportunity to present his conclusions on this side of the Atlantic and to take into account the remarks of American scholars about his general conclusion regarding the effects of industrialization on attitudes toward death. The members of the faculty, students, and guests at Hopkins in April 1973 thus had the opportunity to listen to this outstanding pioneer in the fields of social and cultural history and to discuss his conclusions with him informally after the lectures. There proved to be no language barrier at all: Philippe Ariès speaks English. But master rhetorician that he is, he did not want to diminish the force and eloquence of his spoken words by putting them in what for him is one of his many "second" languages. Thanks to the translations volunteered and stenciled by Patricia M. Ranum, the listeners followed the French with an English text before them. A final thank you also goes to her for giving the time needed to translate the notes and for watching over the lectures every step to their publication as this book.

Orest Ranum

Baltimore
September 1973

Western Attitudes
toward DEATH

Tamed Death

The new behavioral sciences—and linguistics—have introduced the notions of diachrony and synchrony, which will perhaps be helpful to us historians. Since many factors relating to the mentality, or turn of mind, are *long term*, the attitude toward death may appear almost static over very long periods of time. It appears to be a-chronic. And yet, at certain moments, changes occur, usually slow and unnoticed changes, but sometimes, as today, more rapid and perceptible ones. The difficulty for the historian lies in being sensitive to changes, but yet not being obsessed by them to the point of forgetting the great forces of inertia which reduce the real impact of innovations.[1]

With this in mind, I divided the topics under discussion here into four parts. The first chapter is essentially synchronic. It covers a long chain of centuries, approximately a millennium. I have called it: "Tamed Death." In the second chapter we shall encounter diachrony. What changes occurring during the Middle Ages, beginning approximately with the twelfth century, began to modify the a-chronic attitude toward death, and what can be the meaning of these changes? The final two chapters will be devoted to contemporary attitudes, which are reflected in the cult of cemeteries and tombs and in the interdict laid upon death by industrialized societies.

* * *

We shall begin with tamed death. Let us first see how the knights in the *chansons de geste* or the oldest romances faced death.

First of all, they were usually forewarned. They did not die without having had time to realize that

[1]Historians today are discovering the quasi-static nature of traditional cultures. Even their demographic and economic equilibria change little or, when they are upset, tend to return to their habitual state. See the works of E. Le Roy Ladurie, primarily *Les Paysans de Languedoc* (Paris, 1966).

they were going to die. If their deaths were terrible ones, such as by the plague, or abrupt, they had to be presented as the exception, something one did not talk about. Normally, then, the man was forewarned.

"Know ye well," said Gawain, "that I shall not live two days."[2]

King Ban had taken a bad fall. When he regained consciousness, he noticed the crimson blood running from his mouth, his nose, his ears. "He looked up to heaven and uttered as best he could . . . 'Ah, Lord God, help me, for I see and I know that my end has come.' "[3] *I see and I know.*

At Roncevaux, Roland "feels that death is taking hold of him completely. From his head it is moving down toward his heart." "He feels that his time has come."[4] Tristram "sensed that his life was ebbing away, he understood that he was going to die."[5]

---

[2] "La mort d'Artus," *Les romans de la Table ronde*, ed. J. Boulenger (abridged ed.; Paris, 1941), p. 443.

Translator's note: These details are generally not found in Sir Thomas Malory's *Morte d'Arthur*; the author's references to the older French versions of these romances have therefore been used.

[3] "Les enfances de Lancelot du Lac," *ibid.*, p. 124.

[4] *La chanson de Roland*, ed. J. Bédier (Paris, 1922), chaps. CLXXIV, CLXXV, CLXVIII.

[5] *Le roman de Tristan et Iseult*, ed. J. Bédier (Paris, 1946), p. 233.

Pious monks behaved in the same manner as knights. At Saint Martin de Tours, in the tenth century, after four years of seclusion, a venerable hermit "felt," in the words of Raoul Glaber, "that he was soon going to leave this world." The same author recounts how another monk with some medical knowledge had to hurry the brothers he was treating. Time was running out: "He knew that his death was near."[6]

Let us note that the warning came through natural signs or, even more frequently, through an inner conviction rather than through a supernatural, magical premonition. It was something very simple, something prevailing throughout the ages, something which persists even today as an anachronism within industrialized societies. A sort of spontaneous realization, it was foreign both to the cults of the miraculous and to Christian piety. There was no way of cheating, of pretending one hadn't noticed. In 1491, in the midst of the humanist Renaissance which we have the bad habit of contrasting with the Middle Ages—in any event in an urbanized world far different from that of Roland or Tristram—a *juvencula*, a very young girl, pretty, coquettish, loving life and pleasures, was taken ill. Would she, with the complicity of her

---

[6]Quoted by G. Duby, *L'an Mil* (Paris, 1967), p. 89.

intimate friends, cling to life by acting, by pretending that she did not realize the seriousness of her
ailment? No. She did, however, rebel; but this
rebellion did not take the form of a refusal of
death. *"Cum cerneret, infelix juvencula, de prox-
ima situ imminere mortem." Cum cerneret*: She
saw, the wretched girl, her approaching death.
Then, despairing, she offered her soul to the devil.[7]

In the seventeenth century, mad though he was,
Don Quixote made no attempt to flee from death
into the daydreams in which he had passed his life.
On the contrary, the warning signs of death
brought him back to his senses: " 'Niece,' he said
very calmly, 'I feel that death is near.' "[8]

Saint-Simon said that Madame de Montespan
was afraid of death. Actually, she was afraid of not
having a forewarning and also (and we shall return
to this point) of dying alone. "She would go to bed
with all her bed curtains open and a great number
of candles in her room, and women watching about
her whom, whenever she awoke, she expected to
find chatting, playing games, or eating to prevent
themselves from falling asleep." But despite her
anguish, on May 27, 1707, she too knew that she

---

[7]Quoted by A. Tenenti, *Il senso della morte e l'amore della vita nel
Rinascimento* (Turin, 1957), p. 170, n. 18.

[8]Cervantes, *Don Quixote* (Baltimore: Penguin Books, 1950), Part II,
chap. LXXIV, pp. 934–40.

was going to die and made ready.[9] On July 29, 1750, the day of Johann Sebastian Bach's death, Anna Magdalena Bach used the same phrase: ". . . feeling his end approach."[10]

The same words are passed on from age to age, unchanged, like a proverb. We find them in Tolstoy in a period in which their simplicity had already become blurred. But Tolstoy's genius lies in having rediscovered them. On his deathbed in a rural railroad station, Tolstoy murmured: "And the mujiks? How do the mujiks die?" The mujiks died like Roland, Tristram, or Johann Sebastian Bach. They knew what was happening. In Tolstoy's "Three Deaths" an old coachman lies dying in the kitchen of an inn, near the warm brick oven. He knows it. When a woman asks him kindly how he feels, he replies, "It hurts me all over. My death is at hand, that's what it is."[11]

Death still sometimes came like that in the rationalist and positivist, or the romantic and exalted France of the nineteenth century. Take M. Pouget's mother. According to Jean Guitton, "In

[9] Saint-Simon, *Mémoires*, ed. A. de Boislisle (Paris, 1901), Vol. XV, p. 96.

[10] A. M. Bach, *The Little Chronicle*, trans. Esther Meynell (London, 1925).

[11] L. Tolstoi, "Three Deaths," from "The Death of Ivan Ilyitch, and Other Stories," *Works of Lyof N. Tolstoi* (New York, 1899), Vol. XI, p. 81.

1874 she was seized by a *colérine* [a serious illness]. At the end of four days: 'Go get the priest.' The priest came. He wanted to administer the last rites. 'Not yet, Monsieur le Curé, I will notify you when the time comes.' And two days later: 'Go tell Monsieur le Curé to bring me the extreme unction.' " And Jean Guitton—who was writing this in 1941—remarked, "We can see how the Pougets in those bygone days [1874!] passed on from this world into the next, as simple and practical persons, observors of signs and above all of themselves. They were in no hurry to die, but when they saw that their hour had come, then without haste or delay, but with a sense of proper timing, they died as Christians."[12] But non-Christians died just as simply.

* * *

Knowing that his end was near, the dying person prepared for death. And everything would be done very simply, as with the Pougets or Tolstoy's mujiks. In a world as steeped in the supernatural as that of the Round Table, death was a very simple thing. When Launcelot, wounded and dazed in a deserted forest, realized that he had "lost even the

[12] J. Guitton, *Portrait de M. Pouget* (Paris, 1941), p. 14.

strength of his body," he believed he was about to die.[13] So what did he do? His gestures were fixed by old customs, ritual gestures which must be carried out when one is about to die. He removed his weapons and lay down quietly upon the ground, though as last wills and testaments would state over several centuries, he should have been in bed—"*Gisant au lit malade*," lying on my sickbed. He spread his arms out, his body forming a cross—which, too, was not the usual procedure. But he remembered to lie in such a way that his head faced east, toward Jerusalem.

When Iseult found Tristram dead, she knew that she too would die. So she lay down beside him and turned toward the east.

At Roncevaux, Archbishop Turpin awaited his death lying down, and "on his breast, in the very middle, crossed his beautiful white hands." This is the posture of funerary statues beginning with the twelfth century; in primitive Christianity the defunct was portrayed with his arms outstretched, in the manner of a worshipper.

One awaited death lying down, *gisant*. This ritual position was stipulated by the thirteenth-century liturgists. "The dying man," according to Guillaume Durand, bishop of Mende, "must lie on

---

[13] "La quête du Saint Graal," *La Table ronde*, p. 347.

his back so that his face is always turned toward heaven." This posture was not the same as that of the Jews; according to descriptions in the Old Testament, the Jews turned to the wall when dying.

Thus prepared, the dying man could carry out the final steps of the traditional ceremony. Take the example of Roland in the *Chanson de Roland*. The first step was to express sorrow over the end of life, a sad but very discreet recollection of beloved beings and things, a summary which was reduced to a few images. Roland "was seized by several things to remember": first, "of so many lands which he, the valiant one, had conquered," then of sweet France, of the men of his lineage, of Charlemagne, his lord who had nurtured him, of his master and his companions (*compains*). No thought for his mother or his fiancée, just sad, moving recollections. "He wept and could not keep himself from sighing." But this emotion was short-lived, as was the subsequent mourning by the survivors. It was a ritual moment.

After the lamentation about the sadness of dying came the pardoning of the always numerous companions and helpers who surrounded the deathbed. Oliver asked Roland forgiveness for any harm he might have unintentionally done him: " 'I pardon you here and before God.' At these words the one bowed to the other." The dying man commended the survivors to God: " 'May God bless Charles and sweet France,' implored Oliver, 'and above all Roland, my companion.' " In the *Chanson de Roland* the question of a tomb and the selection of its location does not arise. The choice of a tomb does exist however in the later poems of the Round Table.

Now it was time to forget the world and think of God. The prayer had two parts. The first was the *culpa* ("God, by thy grace I admit my guilt for my sins . . ."), which later developed into the *confiteor*. "Oliver confessed his sins aloud, his two hands joined and lifted toward heaven, and begged God to grant him paradise." This was the gesture of the penitent. The second part of the prayer was the *commendacio animae*, a paraphrase of a very old prayer borrowed from the Jewish synagogue. In the French of the sixteenth to eighteenth centuries, these prayers were called the *recommandaces*. "True Father, who never lies, who recalled Lazarus from the dead, who saved Daniel from the lions, save my soul from all peril. . . ."

At this point came absolution, indisputably the sole religious, or rather ecclesiastic (for everything was religious) act. It was granted by the priest, who read psalms, the *libera*, burned incense over the dying man, and sprinkled him with holy water. This absolution was also repeated over the dead body, at the moment of its burial, at which time it was called the *absoute*. But the word *absoute* was never used in common speech; last wills and testaments used the words *les recommandaces*, *le libera*.

Later, in the Romances of the Round Table, the dying received the *Corpus Christi*. Extreme unction was reserved for clerics, especially monks.

After the final prayer all that remained was the wait for death, and there was no reason for death to tarry. Thus Oliver's "heart fails him, his entire body sinks upon the ground. The Count is dead; he lingers no longer." Should death happen to come more slowly, the dying man waited in silence: "He said [his last prayer] and never again uttered a word."[14]

* * *

Let us stop here and make a few general observations. The first—death in bed, the recumbent figure "lying on its sickbed"—has already been sufficiently set forth.

The second is that death was a ritual organized by the dying person himself, who presided over it and knew its protocol. Should he forget or cheat, it

[14] *La chanson de Roland*, chap. CLXVI; Durand de Mende, "Du cimetière . . .," chap. XXXVIII, XXXIV, *Rationale divinorum officiorum*, ed. C. Barthelemy, Paris, 1854, Vol. IV, chap. 5.

was up to those present, the doctor or the priest, to recall him to a routine which was both Christian and customary.

It was also a public ceremony. The dying man's bedchamber became a public place to be entered freely. At the end of the eighteenth century, doctors who were discovering the first principles of hygiene complained about the overcrowded bedrooms of the dying.[15] In the early nineteenth century, passers-by who met the priest bearing the last sacrament still formed a little procession and accompanied him into the sickroom.[16]

It was essential that parents, friends, and neighbors be present. Children were brought in; until the eighteenth century no portrayal of a deathbed scene failed to include children. And to think of how carefully people today keep children away from anything having to do with death!

A final point, and the most important one, is the simplicity with which the rituals of dying were accepted and carried out,—in a ceremonial manner,

[15] "Dès que quelqu'un tombe malade, on ferme la maison, on allume les chandelles et tout le monde s'assemble autour du malade." Enquête médicale organisée par Vicq d'Azyr, 1774-94. J. P. Peter, "Malades et maladies au 18e siècle," *Annales. Économies, sociétés, civilisations*, 1967, p. 712.

[16] P. Craven, *Récit d'une soeur* (Paris, 1867), Vol. II, p. 197. There are numerous portrayals of this scene in the academic paintings of the second half of the nineteenth century.

yes, but with no theatrics, with no great show of emotion.

The best analysis of this attitude is found in Alexander Solzhenitsyn's *The Cancer Ward.* Yefrem thought he knew more about death than the old folk. "The old folk, who never even made it to town, they were scared, while Yefrem rode horses and fired pistols at thirteen. . . . But now . . . he remembered how the old folk used to die back home on the Kama—Russians, Tartars, Votyaks, or whatever they were. They didn't puff themselves up or fight against it and brag that they weren't going to die—they took death *calmly* [author's italics]. They didn't stall squaring things away, they prepared themselves quietly and in good time, deciding who should have the mare, who the foal. . . . And they departed easily, as if they were just moving into a new house."[17]

It could not be better expressed. People had been dying like that for centuries or millennia. In a world of change the traditional attitude toward death appears inert and static. The old attitude in which death was both familiar and near, evoking no great fear or awe, offers too marked a contrast to ours, where death is so frightful that we dare not utter its name. This is why I have called this

[17]A. Solzhenitsyn, *Cancer Ward* (New York, 1969), pp. 96–97.

household sort of death "tamed death." I do not mean that death had once been wild and that it had ceased to be so. I mean, on the contrary, that today it has become wild.

* * *

We shall now touch upon another aspect of the old familiarity with death: the coexistence of the living and the dead.

This is a new and surprising phenomenon, unknown in pagan Antiquity and even in early Christianity. And it has been completely alien to us since the late eighteenth century.

Our knowledge of the ancient pre-Christian civilizations comes in large part from funeral archeology, from objects found in tombs. One of the aims of the ancient funeral cults was to prevent the deceased from *returning* to disturb the living.

Philology provides another insight into ancient beliefs and feelings. The word *funus* can be translated as either the dead body, the funeral ceremony, or murder. *Funestus* means a profanation provoked by a cadaver; in French it became the word *funeste*, or deadly, ill-omened.[18]

---

[18] "Ad sanctos," *Dictionnaire d'archéologie chrétienne* (Paris, 1907), Vol. I, pp. 479ff.

14

Thus, despite their familiarity with death, the Ancients feared being near the dead and kept them at a distance, honoring the sepulchers. The world of the living had to be kept separate from that of the dead. In Rome, the law of the Twelve Tables forbade burial *in urbe*, within the city. The Theodosian Code repeated the same interdict, so that the *sanctitas* of the inhabitants' homes would be preserved. This is why cemeteries were located outside cities, along roads such as the Appian Way of Rome or les Alyscamps of Arles.

St. John Chrysostom experienced the same revulsion as his pagan ancestors when in a homily he directed Christians to oppose a new practice, as yet infrequent: "Watch that you never build a tomb within the city. If a cadaver were placed where you sleep and eat, what protests you would make. And yet you place the dead not near where you sleep and eat, but upon the very limbs of Christ,"[19] that is, in the churches. But the practice denounced by St. John Chrysostom was to spread and become common usage, despite the interdicts of canon law.

This began not so much with Christianity as with the cult of martyrs originating in Africa. Martyrs were buried in extra-urban necropolises

[19] St. John Chrysostom, *Opera . . .*, ed. Montfaucon (Paris, 1718–38), Vol. VII, p. 71, homily 74.

shared by Christians and pagans. The venerated sites of their tombs soon attracted other sepulchers. St. Paulin had his son's body carried to a spot near the martyrs of Aecola in Spain, "so that he might be associated with the martyrs through the union of the tomb, in order that in the vicinity of the blood of the saints he may draw upon that virtue which purifies our souls against fire."[20] "The martyrs," explained another fifth-century author, Maximus of Turin, "will keep guard over us, who live with our bodies, and they will take us into their care when we have forsaken our bodies. Here they prevent us from falling into sinful ways, there they will protect us from the horrors of hell. That is why our ancestors were careful to unite our bodies with the bones of the martyrs."[21]

This union began in the extra-urban cemeteries where the first martyrs had been buried. Over the saint's tomb a basilica would be built and entrusted to monks. Christians sought to be buried close to this structure. Diggings in the Roman cities of Africa or Spain reveal an extraordinary spectacle concealed by subsequent urban growth: piles of stone sarcophagi in disorder, one on top of the other, several layers high, especially around the

[20] "Ad sanctos," *Dictionnaire d'archéologie chrétienne*, Vol. I, pp. 479ff.

[21] *Patrologia latina*, Vol. LVII, cols. 427–28.

walls of the apse, close to the shrine of the saint. This accumulation bears witness to the desire to be buried near the saints, *ad sanctos.*

A time came when the distinction disappeared between the suburbs, where people were buried *ad sanctos* because the site was *extra urbem*, and the city, where tombs had always been forbidden. We know how this occurred at Amiens in the sixth century. St. Vaast, a bishop who died in 540, had selected his tomb outside the city. But when the pallbearers tried to carry him away they could not move the corpse, which had suddenly become too heavy. Then the archpriest begged the saint to command "that you be carried to the spot which we [the clergy of the cathedral] have prepared for you"[22] within the church. He was correctly interpreting the saint's wishes, for the body at once became light. In order for the clergy to circumvent the traditional interdict and to make provision within the cathedral for the tombs of the saints and the sepulchers which the holy tomb would attract, the old revulsion would already have had to become much weakened.

Thus, the distinction between the abbey with its cemetery and the cathedral church became blurred.

[22] Quoted in E. Salin, *La civilisation mérovingienne* (Paris, 1949–59), Vol. II, p. 35.

The dead, which already mingled with the inhabitants of the popular quarters that had been built in the suburbs about the abbeys, also made their way into the historic heart of the cities from which they had been excluded for thousands of years.

Henceforth, there would be no difference between the church and the cemetery.

* * *

In medieval speech the word "church" did not mean solely the church buildings but the entire space around the church. In the customary law of Hainault the "parochial" or parish church included the nave, the belfrey, and the *"chimiter"* or cemetery.

Sermons were preached, sacraments were distributed on high holy days, and processions were held within the courtyard or *atrium* of the church, which was also hallowed ground. Reciprocally, people were buried either in the church, against its walls, in the surrounding area (*in porticu*), or under the rain spouts (*sub stillicidio*). The word cemetery was more specifically used for the outer part of the church, the *atrium*, or in French the *aitre*. *Aitre* was one of two words used in common speech to designate the cemetery, for until the fifteenth cen-

tury the word cemetery belonged to the Latin of
the clerics.[23] Turpin urged Roland in the *Chanson
de Roland* to sound his horn so that the king and
his army could come to avenge them, weep over
them, and "bury them in the *aitres* of the monas-
teries." The word *aitre* has disappeared from
modern French, but its Germanic equivalent has
persisted in English, German, and Dutch as
"churchyard."

In French another word was used as a synonym
for *aitre*: the *charnier* or charnel house. In the
Chanson de Roland it appears as *carnier*. It has
persisted, in its most primitive form, the form
which is closest to the Latin word *carnis*, in
popular French slang: "*une vieille carne*," an old
nag or a tough piece of meat; and it probably was,
in Roland's day, a sort of slang term for something
for which classical Latin had no name and which
church Latin had christened with the scholarly
Greek word *cimeterium*. It is interesting to note
that for the Romans the funeral structure itself—
tumulus, sepulcrum, monumentum, or more simply *loculus*—was more important than the space it

[23] C. Du Cange, "Cemeterium," *Glossarium mediae et infimae latini-
tatis* (Niort, 1883–87); E. Viollet-le-Duc, "Tombeau," *Dictionnaire
raisonnée de l'architecture française* (Paris, 1870), Vol. IX, pp.
21–67; *La chanson de Roland*, chap. CXXXII.

occupied. To the medieval mind, on the contrary, the enclosed space about the sepulchers was more important than the tomb itself.

In the beginning *charnier* or charnel house was synonymous with *aitre*. By the end of the Middle Ages it meant only a part of the cemetery, that is to say the galleries which ran along the churchyard and above which were ossuaries. In fifteenth-century Paris, the Cemetery of the Innocents "is a great cemetery, a very large enclosure of houses called *charniers*, in which the dead are piled up."[24]

Thus we can imagine the cemetery as it appeared in the Middle Ages and even into the sixteenth and seventeenth centuries, until the Age of the "Enlightenment."

It was a rectangular churchyard, with the church itself generally forming one of its four sides. The three others were often decorated with arcades or charnel houses. Above these galleries were the ossuaries in which skulls and limbs were artistically arranged. This striving after artistic effects with bones—a form of decoration which was both baroque and macabre—ended in the mid-eighteenth century; examples can still be seen in Rome in the Capuchin Church or in the church which stands

[24]G. Le Breton, *Description de Paris sous Charles VI*, quoted in J. Leroux de Lincy and L. Tisserand, *Paris et ses historiens* (Paris, 1867), p. 193.

"The Cemetery of the Innocents and Its Charnel House,
Paris, during the reign of Francis I" (sixteenth-century
Flemish), in the Musée Carnavalet, Paris. Photo Lauros-
Giraudon.

behind the Farnese Palace, where chandeliers and ornaments are made solely of small bones.

Where did the bones thus displayed in the charnel houses come from? They came chiefly from the great common graves—called the *fosses aux pauvres*, the ditches for the poor. Several yards deep and wide, they were gradually filled up with cadavers sewn into their shrouds. When one ditch was full it was covered with earth, an old one was reopened, and the bones were taken to the charnel houses. The remains of the more wealthy dead, buried within the church itself, were not placed in vaults but in the dirt, under the flagstones. They too eventually followed the path to the charnel houses. As yet unborn was the modern idea that the dead person should be installed in a sort of house unto himself, a house of which he was the perpetual owner or at least the long-term tenant, a house in which he would be at home and from which he could not be evicted. In the Middle Ages and even as late as the sixteenth and seventeenth centuries the exact destination of one's bones was of little concern so long as they remained near the saints, or in the church, near the altar of the Virgin or of the Holy Sacrament. Thus the body was entrusted to the Church. It made little difference what the Church saw fit to do with these bodies so long as they remained within its holy precincts.

* * *

The fact that the dead had entered the church and its courtyard did not prevent both from becoming public places. The use of the cemetery for non-funeral purposes developed from the notion that it was an asylum and a refuge. For the lexicographer Charles Du Cange (1610–88) the word *cimetière* did not always necessarily denote the place of burials; it could also mean a place of asylum independent of any funeral usage. He defined cemetery in terms of the notion of asylum: *Azylus circum ecclesiam.*[25]

Thus, within this asylum called a cemetery, whether or not bodies were buried there, people began to reside, to build houses, and then the word "cemetery" came to mean, if not a quarter of the city, at least a cluster of houses enjoying certain fiscal or domanial privileges. More broadly speaking, people became accustomed to meeting within this asylum, as had the Romans in the Forum or the Mediterraneans on the Plaza Major or the Corso, in order to carry on business, to dance and gamble, or simply for the pleasure of being to-

[25] Du Cange, "Cemeterium"; E. Lesnes, "Les cimetières," *Histoire de la propriété ecclésiastique en France* (Lille, 1910), Vol. III; A. Bernard, *La sépulture en droit canonique* (Paris, 1933); C. Enlart, *Manuel d'archéologie médiévale* (Paris, 1927), p. 909.

gether. Shops and merchants appeared along the charnel houses. Within the Cemetery of the Innocents public scribes offered their services.

In 1231 the Church Council of Rouen forbade dancing in cemeteries or churches under pain of excommunication. Another council held in 1405 forbade dancing in cemeteries, forbade carrying on any form of gambling there, and forbade mummers and jugglers, theatrical troops, musicians, and charlatans to carry on their doubtful trades there.

A text dated 1657 reveals that people were beginning to be disturbed by the juxtaposition in a single place of tombs and "five hundred sorts of sports which can be seen within these galleries." "In the midst of this throng [of public writers, seamstresses, booksellers, second-hand clothes dealers] people had to go about conducting a burial, reopening a tomb, and removing cadavers which were not yet entirely decomposed; here, even in the dead of winter, the earth of the cemetery gave off mephitic odors."[26] But although at the end of the seventeenth century signs of intolerance began to appear, the fact remains that for more than a thousand years people had been perfectly adapted

[26]Berthold, *La ville de Paris en vers burlesques. Journal d'un voyage à Paris en 1657*, quoted in V. Dufour, *Paris à travers les âges* (Paris, 1875–82), Vol. II.

to this promiscuity between the living and the dead.

The spectacle of the dead, whose bones were always being washed up to the surface of the cemeteries, as was the skull in *Hamlet*, made no more impression upon the living than did the idea of their own death. They were as familiar with the dead as they were familiarized with the idea of their own death.

One's Own Death

We have seen how Western civilization had adopted a sort of vulgate of death. Today we shall see that this vulgate was not abandoned or blotted out, but instead was partially altered during the second Middle Ages, that is to say beginning with the eleventh and twelfth centuries. I want to stress from the outset that this was not a matter of a new attitude which took the place of the preceding one, which we have just analyzed; but rather subtle modifications gradually gave a dramatic and personal meaning to man's traditional familiarity with death.

In order to understand properly these phenomena we must keep in mind the fact that this traditional familiarity implied a collective notion of destiny. Men of that period were profoundly and rapidly socialized. The family did not intervene to delay the socialization of the child. Moreover, socialization did not separate man from nature, with which he could not interfere short of a miracle. Familiarity with death is a form of acceptance of the order of nature, an acceptance which can be both naive, in day-to-day affairs, and learned, in astrological speculations.

In death man encountered one of the great laws of the species, and he had no thought of escaping it or glorifying it. He merely accepted it with just the proper amount of solemnity due one of the important thresholds which each generation always had to cross.

This brings us to an analysis of a series of new phenomena which introduced the concern for the individuality of each person into the old idea of the collective destiny of the species. The phenomena we have selected are (1) the portrayal of the Last Judgment at the end of the world; (2) the displacing of this judgment to the end of each life, to the precise moment of death; (3) macabre themes and the interest shown in portrayals of physical decomposition; and (4) the return to fu-

neral inscriptions and to a certain personalization of
tombs.

THE PORTRAYAL OF THE LAST JUDGMENT

In about 680 Bishop Agilbert was buried in the
funeral chapel which he had had constructed adjacent to the monastery of Jouarre (Seine-et-Marne),
to which he had retired and where he died. His
tomb is still standing. What do we find there? On a
small panel is the Christ in Majesty surrounded by
the four Evangelists. This is the image inspired by
the Apocalypse, of Christ returning at the end of
the world. On the large panel adjoining it we find
the resurrection of the dead on the last day. The
elect, their arms upraised, acclaim the returning
Christ, who holds in his hands a scroll, no doubt
the Book of Life.[1] No judgment or condemnation
is in evidence. This image is in keeping with the
general eschatology of the early centuries of Chris-
tendom. The dead who belonged to the Church
and who had entrusted their bodies to its care (that
is to say to the care of the saints), went to sleep
like the seven sleepers of Ephesus (*pausantes, in*

---

[1] J. Hubert, *Les cryptes de Jouarre* (IVe Congrès de l'art du haut
moyen-âge) (Melun: Imprimerie de la préfecture de Seine-et-Marne,
1952).

29

Tomb of the Venerable Agilbert, bishop of Dorchester and Paris, in the crypt of St. Paul's Church, Jouarre. Photo Giraudon.

somno pacis) and were at rest (*requiescant*) until
the day of the Second Coming, of the great return,
when they would awaken in the heavenly Jerusalem, in other words in Paradise. There was no
place for individual responsibility, for a counting
of good and bad deeds. The wicked, that is to say
those who were not members of the Church, would
doubtlessly not live after their death; they would
not awaken and would be abandoned to a state of
nonexistence. An entire quasi-biological population, the saintly population, thus would be granted
a glorious afterlife following a long, expectant
sleep.

But in the twelfth century the scene changed. In
the sculptured tympana of the romanesque
churches of Beaulieu or Conques the apocalyptic
vision of the Majesty of Christ still predominates.
But beneath the portrayal of Christ appears a new
iconography, inspired this time by the book of
Matthew: the resurrection of the dead, the separation of the just and the damned, the Last Judgment (at Conques, Christ's halo bears the word
Judex), and the weighing of souls by the archangel
Michael.[2]

In the thirteenth century[3] the apocalyptic in-
spiration and the evocation of the Second Coming

[2] Tympana of Beaulieu, Conques, Autun.

[3] Tympana of the cathedrals of Paris, Bourges, Bordeaux, Amiens,
etc.

were almost blotted out. The idea of the judgment won out and the scene became a court of justice. Christ is shown seated upon the judgment throne surrounded by his court (the apostles). Two acts had become increasingly important: the weighing of souls and the intercession of the Virgin and St. John, who kneel, their hands clasped, on either side of Christ the Judge. Each man is to be judged according to the balance sheet of his life. Good and bad deeds are scrupulously separated and placed on the appropriate side of the scales. Moreover, these deeds have been inscribed in a book. In the magnificent strains of the *Dies irae* the Franciscan authors of the thirteenth century portrayed the book being brought before the judge on the last day, a book in which everything is inscribed and on the basis of which everyone will be judged.

> *Liber scriptus proferetur*
> *In quo totum continetur*
> *Unde mundus judicetur.*

This book, the *liber vitae*, must first have been conceived of as a cosmic book, the formidable census of the universe. But at the end of the Middle Ages it became an individual account book. At Albi, in the vast fresco of the Last Judgment dating from the end of the fifteenth or the beginning of the sixteenth century,[4] the risen wear this book about their necks, like a passport, or rather like a bank book to be presented at the gates of eternity. A very curious change has occurred. This "balance" (*balancia*) or balance sheet is closed not at the moment of death but on the *dies illa*, the last day of the world, at the end of time. Here we can see the deep-rooted refusal to link the end of physical being with physical decay. Men of the period believed in an existence after death which did not necessarily continue for infinite eternity, but which provided an extension between death and the end of the world.

Thus, the idea of the Last Judgment is linked with that of the individual biography, but this biography ends on the last day, and not at the hour of death.

IN THE BEDCHAMBER OF THE DYING

The second phenomenon consisted of suppressing the eschatological time between death and the end of the world, and of no longer situating the judgment in space at the Second Coming, but in the bedchamber, around the deathbed.

[4] At the rear of the apse.

This new inconography is to be found in the woodcuts, spread by the new technique of printing, in books which are treatises on the proper manner of dying: the *artes moriendi* of the fifteenth and sixteenth centuries.[5] Nonetheless, this iconography brings us back to the traditional image of the deathbed which we studied in the first chapter.

The dying man is lying in bed surrounded by his friends and relations. He is in the process of carrying out the rituals which are now familiar to us. But something is happening which disturbs the simplicity of the ceremony and which those present do not see. It is a spectacle reserved for the dying man alone and one which he contemplates with a bit of anxiety and a great deal of indifference. Supernatural beings have invaded his chamber and cluster about the bed of the recumbent figure, the "*gisant*." On one side are the Trinity, the Virgin, and the celestial court; on the other, Satan and a monstrous army of demons. Thus the great gathering which in the twelfth and thirteenth centuries had taken place on the last day, in the fifteenth century had moved to the sickroom.

How are we to interpret this scene?

---

[5] Texts and woodcuts of an *Ars moriendi* reproduced in A. Tenenti, *La vie et la mort à travers le XVe siècle* (Paris, 1952), pp. 97–120.

"St. Sebastian Interceding for the Plague-stricken"
(1497–99), by Josse Lieferinxe, in the Walters Art Gal-
lery, Baltimore. Reproduced by permission of the
Walters Art Gallery.

Is it still really a judgment? Properly speaking, no. The scales in which good and evil are weighed no longer play a part. The book is still present, and all too frequently the demon has grabbed it with a triumphant gesture, because the account book and the person's life story are in his favor. But God no longer appears with the attributes of a judge. In the two possible interpretations, interpretations which probably can be superimposed, God is rather the arbiter or the observer.

The first interpretation is that of a cosmic struggle between the forces of good and evil who are fighting for possession of the dying man, and the dying man himself watches this battle as an impartial witness, though he is the prize.

This interpretation is suggested by the graphic composition of this scene in the woodcuts of the *artes moriendi*. But if one reads carefully the inscriptions that accompany these woodcuts one will see that they deal with a different matter, which is the second interpretation. God and his court are there to observe how the dying man conducts himself during this trial—a trial he must endure before he breathes his last and which will determine his fate in eternity. This test consists of a final temptation. The dying man will see his entire life as it is contained in the book, and he will be tempted either by despair over his sins, by the "vainglory" of his good deeds, or by the passionate love for things and persons. His attitude during this fleeting moment will erase at once all the sins of his life if he wards off tempation or, on the contrary, will cancel out all his good deeds if he gives way. The final test has replaced the Last Judgment.

Here we must make two important observations.

The first concerns the juxtaposition of the traditional portrayal of death in bed and that of the individual judgment of each life. Death in bed, as we have seen, was a calming rite which solemnized the necessary passing, the "*trépas*," and leveled the differences between individuals. No one worried about the fate of one particular dying man. Death would come to him as it did to all men, or rather to all Christians at peace with the Church. It was an essentially collective rite.

On the other hand, the judgment—even though it took place in a great cosmic activity at the end of the world—was peculiar to each individual, and no one knew his fate until the judge had weighed the souls, heard the pleas of intercessors, and made his decision.

Thus the iconography of the *artes moriendi* joins in a single scene the security of a collective rite and the anxiety of a personal interrogation.

My second observation concerns the increasingly close relationship established between death and the biography of each individual life. It took time for this relationship to gain ascendency. In the fourteenth and fifteenth centuries it became firmly fixed, no doubt under the influence of the mendicant orders. From then on it was thought that each person's entire life flashed before his eyes at the moment of death. It was also believed that his attitude at that moment would give his biography its final meaning, its conclusion.

Thus we understand how the ritual solemnity of the deathbed, which persisted into the nineteenth century, by the end of the Middle Ages had assumed among the educated classes a dramatic character, an emotional burden which it had previously lacked.

We must, however, note that this evolution strengthened the role played by the dying man himself in the ceremonies surrounding his own death. He was still at the center of activity, presiding over the event as in the past, and determining the ritual as he saw fit.

These ideas were bound to change in the seventeenth and eighteenth centuries. Under the influence of the Counter Reformation, spiritual writers struggled against the popular belief that it was not necessary to take such pains to live virtuously, since a good death redeemed everything. However,

they continued to acknowledge that there was a
moral importance in the way the dying man behaved and in the circumstances surrounding his
death. It was not until the twentieth century that
this deeply rooted belief was cast off, at least in
industrialized societies.

THE "TRANSI," OR WORM-RIDDEN CORPSE

The third phenomenon appears during the same
period as the *artes moriendi*: this is the appearance
in art and literature of the cadaver, called the
"*transi*" (the perished one) or the "*charogne*" (the
carrion).[6]

We must point out that in the art of the fourteenth to sixteenth centuries the portrayal of death
in the form of a mummy, of a partly decomposed
cadaver, was less widespread than is thought. It is
found chiefly in the fifteenth-century illuminated
manuscripts of the Service for the Dead, and in the
decoration of churches and cemeteries (the Dance
of Death). It is much rarer in funeral art. The sub-

---

[6]*Ibid.*; A. Tenenti, *Il senso della morte et l'amore della vita nel
Rinascimento* (Turin, 1957), pp. 139–84; and J. Huizinga, *The
Waning of the Middle Ages* (London, 1924), chap. XI, "The Vision
of Death," pp. 138–50.

stitution of a cadaver or *transi* for the recumbent figure or *gisant* was limited to certain regions such as eastern France and western Germany, and is rarely found in Italy and Spain. It was never really accepted as a common theme for funeral art. Later, in the seventeenth century, the skeleton or bones, and not the decomposing cadaver, were to be found on nearly every tomb and even found their way into houses, on fireplaces and furniture. But the vulgarization after the late sixteenth century of macabre objects, in the form of a skull or bones, has a meaning different from that of the putrified cadaver.

Historians have been struck by the appearance of the cadaver and the mummy in iconography. The great Huizinga saw it as a proof of his thesis about the moral crisis during the "waning of the Middle Ages." Today Tenenti sees instead in this horror of death the sign of the love of life (*"la vie pleine"*) and of the overthrow of the Christian scheme of life. My interpretation would be in the direction of Tenenti's.

Before proceeding further, we must point out a significant omission in last wills and testaments of this period. Testators of the fifteenth century referred to their *charogne*, their "carrion," but the word disappeared in the sixteenth century. Nevertheless, in general the death portrayed in wills was related to the peaceful conception of death in bed. The horror of physical death, of which the cadaver could be considered a sign, was completely absent, which leads us to assume that it was also absent from the common mentality.

On the other hand, and this is a very important observation, the horror of physical death and of decomposition is a familiar theme in fifteenth- and sixteenth-century poetry. "*Sac à fiens*" (*fientes*), "bag of droppings," said P. de Nesson (1383–1442).

> O carrion, who art no longer man,
> Who will hence keep thee company?
> Whatever issues from thy liquors,
> Worms engendered by the stench
> Of thy vile carrion flesh.[7]

But this horror was not restricted to *post-mortem* decomposition; it was *intra vitem*, in illness, in old age:

[7]"O charoigne, qui n'es mais hon,/Qui te tenra lors compaignée?/Ce qui istra [sortira] de ta liqueur,/Vers engendrés de la pueur/De ta vile chair encharoignée."

Pierre de Nesson, "Vigiles des morts: Paraphrase sur Job," quoted in *Anthologie poétique française, Moyen-Âge*, ed. Garnier (Paris, 1967), Vol. II, p. 184.

> I am nothing but bones, I seem a skeleton,
> Fleshless, muscleless, pulpless . . .
> My body is diminishing to the point where
> everything becomes disjointed.[8]

Here we are not dealing with moralizing intentions, with the arguments of preachers. These poets are aware of the universal presence of corruption. It is present in cadavers but also in the midst of life, in "*les oeuvres naturelles*," the operations of nature. The worms which devour cadavers do not come from the earth but from within the body, from its natural "liquors."

> Each conduit [of the body]
> Constantly produces putrid matter
> Out of the body.[9]

Decomposition is the sign of man's failure, and that is undoubtedly the underlying meaning of the

---

[8] "Je n'ay plus que les os, un squelette je semble/décharné, démusclé, dépoulpé . . ./Mon corps s'en va descendre où tout se désassemble."

P. de Ronsard, "Derniers vers," Sonnet I, *Oeuvres complètes*, ed. P. Laumonier (rev. ed.; Paris: Silver and Le Bègue, 1967), Vol. XVIII, Part 1, pp. 176–77.

[9] "Chascun conduit [du corps]/Puante matière produit/Hors du corps continuellement."

Pierre de Nesson, quoted in A. Tenenti, *Il senso della morte*, p. 147.

Detail from "St. George Fighting the Dragon," by Vittore Carpaccio, in Scuola de S. Giorgio degli Schiavoni in Venice. Photo Anderson-Giraudon, Rome.

macabre, which turns this failure into a new and original phenomenon.

In order better to understand this phenomenon, we must cast aside the contemporary notion of failure which is, alas, very familiar to us in today's industrialized societies.

Today the adult experiences sooner or later—and increasingly it is sooner—the feeling that he has failed, that his adult life has failed to achieve any of the promises of his adolescence. This feeling is at the basis of the climate of depression which is spreading throughout the leisured classes of industrialized societies.

This feeling was completely foreign to the mentalities of traditional societies, those in which one died like Roland or Tolstoy's peasants. But it was no longer foreign to the rich, powerful, or learned man of the late Middle Ages. Nevertheless there is a very interesting difference between our contemporary feeling of personal failure and that found in the late Middle Ages. The certainty of death and the fragility of life are foreign to our existential pessimism.

On the contrary the man of the late Middle Ages was very acutely conscious that he had merely been granted a stay of execution, that this delay would be a brief one, and that death was always present within him, shattering his ambitions and poisoning his pleasures. And that man felt a love of life which we today can scarcely understand, perhaps because of our increased longevity.

"We must leave behind our house, our orchards, and our gardens, dishes and vessels which the artisan engraved," wrote Ronsard, reflecting upon death.[10] Which of us faced with death would weep over a house in Florida or a farm in Virginia? In proto-capitalist eras—in other words, in periods when the capitalist and technological mentality was being developed, the process would not be completed until the eighteenth century—man had an unreasoning, visceral love for *temporalia*, which was a blanket word including things, men, and animals.

We now reach a point in our analysis where we can reach a general conclusion about these first few phenomena we have observed: the Last Judgment, the final trial of the *artes moriendi*, and the love of life evidenced in macabre themes. During the second half of the Middle Ages, from the twelfth to the fifteenth centuries, three categories of mental images were brought together: the image of death, that of the individual's knowledge of his

---

[10]"Il faut laisser maisons, et vergers, et jardins/Vaisselles et vaisseaux que l'artisan burine . . . ."

Ronsard, "Derniers vers," Sonnet XI, *Oeuvres complètes*, Vol. XVIII, Part 1, p. 180.

own biography, and that of the passionate attachment for things and creatures possessed during
one's lifetime. Death became the occasion when
man was most able to reach an awareness of himself.

TOMBS

The last phenomenon remaining to be studied confirms this general trend. It concerns the tombs, or
to be more exact, the individualization of sepulchers.[11]

We cannot be very much in error in saying that,
in Ancient Rome, everyone, even the slaves, had a
burial place, a *loculus*, and that this place was
marked by an inscription. Countless funeral inscriptions have been uncovered. They were still numerous at the beginning of the Christian era, indicating
the desire to preserve the identity of the tomb.

Beginning with the fifth century such inscriptions became rare and disappeared more or less
rapidly according to the locality. In addition to the
name of the deceased, stone sarcophagi had often
included his portrait. The portraits disappeared in
their turn so that the sepulchers became com-

[11] E. Panofski, *Tomb Sculpture* (London, 1964).

pletely anonymous. This evolution should not surprise us after my earlier discussion of burial *ad sanctos*: the dead person was given over to the Church, which took care of him until the Resurrection Day. The cemeteries of the first half of the Middle Ages, and even cemeteries of later times where older customs persisted, are accumulations of stone, sometimes sculptured, almost always anonymous, so that, unless funeral furnishings are to be found, it is difficult to date them.

However, beginning with the thirteenth century—and perhaps slightly earlier—we again find the funeral inscriptions which had all but disappeared during the previous eight or nine hundred years.

They reappeared first on the tombs of illustrious personages—that is to say of saints or those associated with the saints. These tombs, at first very rare, became more frequent as the thirteenth century progressed. The funeral slab of Queen Mathilda, the first queen of Norman England, bears a brief inscription.

With the inscription the effigy also reappeared, without being a true portrait. It evoked the beatified or elected person awaiting Paradise. However, during the reign of Louis IX of France it became increasingly realistic and attempted to reproduce the features of the living person. Finally, in the fourteenth century, realism was carried to the point of reproducing a death mask. For a certain category of illustrious personages, both clergy and lay—the only persons to have great sculpted tombs—there was thus a development from complete anonymity, to a short inscription, and finally to a realistic portrait. The evolution in funeral art forms continued on the way to increased personalization until the early seventeenth century, and the dead person might be portrayed twice on the same tomb, both alive and dead.

These monumental tombs are very familiar to us, because they belong to the history of art and of sculpture. In reality they are not numerous enough to constitute a basic element of our civilization. But they provide us with a few indications that the general evolution followed the same direction.

Alongside the great monumental tombs we see in the thirteenth century an increase in little plaques about 30 to 40 centimeters wide which were affixed to interior or exterior walls of the church or to a pillar. These plaques are relatively unknown because they have been neglected by art historians. Most of them have disappeared. They are, however, very interesting to the historian of mentalities, for they were the most common form of funeral monuments until the eighteenth century. Some were simple inscriptions in Latin or

French: "Here lies John Doe, who died on such and such a day," and then his occupation. Others, which were somewhat larger, included in addition to the inscription a scene in which the deceased person was portrayed either alone or most commonly before Christ or beside a religious scene. These wall plaques were very common in the sixteenth, seventeenth, and eighteenth centuries. They reveal the desire to render the burial place individual and to perpetuate the memory of the deceased in that spot.[12]

In the eighteenth century, tombs with a simple inscription became increasingly numerous, at least in the cities, where artisans—the middle class of that period—were eager in their turn to leave anonymity behind and preserve their identity after death.[13]

Nevertheless, these tombstone plaques were not the only way nor perhaps the most widespread way of perpetuating the memory of the deceased. In their wills the deceased themselves provided for perpetual religious services for the salvation of their soul. Beginning with the thirteenth century and continuing until the eighteenth century, the

[12] Numerous "*tableaux*" or plaques exist in the chapel of St. Hilaire at Marville in the French Ardennes.

[13] For example, at Toulouse in the cloister of the Jacobins: the tomb of X, master cooper, and his family.

testators or their heirs would have the terms of their donation and the obligations of the *curé* and the parish engraved on a stone plaque. These donation plaques were at least as important as those bearing a "Here lies." Sometimes both elements were present. Sometimes the donation plaque was considered sufficient and the "Here lies" was omitted. The important element was the calling to mind of the deceased's identity, and not the remembrance of the exact place where the body had been placed.[14]

* * *

The study of tombs confirms what we have learned from the Last Judgments, the *artes*

---

[14] For example, a "*tableau*" serving as a reminder of a bequest in the church of Andrésy, near Pontoise. At the top are the donor's arms, followed by the inscription:

"À la gloire de Dieu, à la mémoire des cinq playes de N[ostre] S[eigneur] J[ésus] C[hrist].

"Claude Le Page, escuyer, sieur de la Chapelle, ancien conducteur de la Haquenée, chef du gobelet du Roi, ancien valet de chambre garde robe de feu Monsieur, frère unique de S[a] M[ajesté] Louis 14, lequel il a servi quatre huit années, jusqu'à son deceds et a depuis continué le même service près monsaigneur le Duc d'Orléans son fils, a *fondé à perpétuité* pour le repos de son âme, de ses parens et amis, tous les mois de l'année une messe le 6 de chaque mois en la chapelle de Saint Jean dont l'une sera haute, le jour de S[t.] Claude, auxquelles assisteront 5 pauvres et un garçon pour répondre aux dites messes, à qui les Marguilliers donneront à chacun des six 5 liards dont ils en porteront un à l'offrande.

moriendi, and the macabre themes: Beginning with
the eleventh century a formerly unknown relationship developed between the death of each individual and his awareness of being an individual. Today
it is agreed that between the year 1000 and the
middle of the thirteenth century "a very important
historical mutation occurred," as a contemporary
medievalist, Pacault, expressed it. "The manner in
which men applied their thoughts to their sur-
roundings and to their concerns underwent a profound transformation, while the mental proc-
esses—the manner of reasoning, of perceiving con-
crete or abstract realities, and of conceiving ideas—
evolved radically."[15]

Here we can grasp this change in the mirror of
death or, in the words of the old authors, in the
speculum mortis. In the mirror of his own death
each man would discover the secret of his indi-

"Le tout accordé par Messieurs les curés, marguilliers en charge et
anciens de la paroisse S[t.] Germain d'Andrésy, ce qui est plus
amplement expliqué par le contrat passé le 27 janvier 1703 par
devant M^e [maîtres] Bailly et Desfforges, notaires au Châtelet de
Paris.

"Cette épitaphe a esté placée par le soin du fondateur, aagé de
soixante dix-neuf ans le 24 janvier 1704."

A different hand subsequently engraved: "et décédé le 24 décembre
de la même année."

[15] M. Pacault, "De l'aberration à la logique: essai sur les mutations
de quelques structures ecclésiastiques," *Revue historique*, Vol.
CCXXXXII (1972), p. 313.

viduality. And this relationship—which Greco-Roman Antiquity, and especially Epicurianism, had glimpsed briefly and had then lost—has from that time on never ceased to make an impression on our Western civilization. With little difficulty the man of traditional societies, the man of the first Middle Ages which we studied in our preceding lecture, became resigned to the idea that we are all mortal. Since the High Middle Ages Western man has come to see himself in his own death: he has discovered *la mort de soi*, one's own death.

Thy Death

Thus far we have illustrated two attitudes toward death. The first, the oldest, the longest held, and the most common one, is the familiar resignation to the collective destiny of the species and can be summarized by the phrase, *Et morie-mur*, and we shall all die. The second, which appeared in the twelfth century, reveals the importance given throughout the entire modern period to the self, to one's own existence, and can be expressed by another phrase, *la mort de soi*, one's own death.

Beginning with the eighteenth century, man in western societies tended to give death a new meaning. He exalted it, dramatized it, and thought of it as disquieting and greedy. But he already was less concerned with his own death than with *la mort de toi*, the death of the other person, whose loss and memory inspired in the nineteenth and twentieth centuries the new cult of tombs and cemeteries and the romantic, rhetorical treatment of death.

* * *

A major phenomenon occurred between the sixteenth and eighteenth centuries, a phenomenon which we must touch upon here, even if we do not analyze it in detail. This phenomenon did not occur in the world of real, acted-out events which the historian can easily collect and measure. It occurred in the obscure and extravagant world of phantasms, and the historian studying it ought to transform himself into a psychoanalyst.

At the end of the fifteenth century, we see the themes concerning death begin to take on an erotic meaning. In the oldest dances of death, Death scarcely touched the living to warn him and designate him. In the new iconography of the sixteenth century, Death raped the living.[1] From the six-

---

[1] For example, the paintings by Hans Baldung Grien (d. 1545), "Rider with Death and a Maiden," in the Louvre, and "Death and the Woman," in the museum of Basel.

teenth to the eighteenth centuries, countless scenes or motifs in art and in literature associate death with love, Thanatos with Eros. These are erotico-macabre themes, or simply morbid ones, which reveal extreme complaisance before the spectacles of death, suffering, and torture. Athletic, nude executioners strip the skin from St. Bartholomew. When Bernini portrayed the mystic union of St. Theresa of Avila with God, he juxtaposed the images of the death agony and the orgasmic trance. The baroque theater staged its love scenes in tombs, such as that of the Capulets.[2] The macabre literature of the eighteenth century united the young monk to the dead beauty over whom he was keeping watch.[3]

Like the sexual act, death was henceforth increasingly thought of as a transgression which tears man from his daily life, from rational society, from his monotonous work, in order to make him undergo a paroxysm, plunging him into an irrational, violent, and beautiful world. Like the sexual act death for the Marquis de Sade is a break, a rupture. This idea of rupture is something completely

[2] J. Rousset, *La littérature de l'âge baroque en France* (Paris, 1954).

[3] An oft-quoted anecdote told by Doctor Louis, "Lettre sur l'incertitude des signes de la mort," 1752, found in Foederé's article, "Signes de la mort," *Dictionnaire des Sciences médicales* (Paris, 1818), Vol. LI.

new. Until this point the stress had been on the familiarity with death and with the dead. This familiarity had not been affected, even for the rich and the mighty, by the upsurge of individualism beginning in the twelfth century. Death had become a more important event; more thought had to be given to it. But it had become neither frightening nor obsessive. It had remained familiar and tamed.

But from now on it would be thought of as a *break*.[4]

This notion of a break was born and developed in the world of erotic phantasms. It then passed into the world of real and acted-out events.

Of course, at that point it lost its erotic characteristics, or at least they were sublimated and reduced to Beauty. Death was no longer desirable, as in the macabre novels, but it was admirable in its beauty. This is what would be called the romantic death, found in Lamartine in France, the Bronte family in England, and Mark Twain in America.

We have many literary examples of this. Lamartine's "Méditations poétiques" are meditations on death. We also have a great number of memoirs and letters. During the 1840s a French family, the de La Ferronays, was decimated by

[4]G. Bataille, *L'érotisme* (Paris, 1957).

tuberculosis. One survivor, Pauline Craven, published the intimate diaries and correspondence of
her brothers, sisters, and parents, most of which
were narratives of illnesses, death agonies, deaths,
and thoughts about death.[5]

Of course, in many ways these memoirs recall
the old customs. The ceremony of death in bed,
presided over by the dying person surrounded by a
crowd of relatives and friends, persists and still provides the framework for the setting. But it is at
once obvious that something has changed.

In the past death in bed was a solemn event, but
also an event as banal as seasonal holidays. People
expected it, and when it occurred they followed
the rituals laid down by custom. But in the nineteenth century, a new passion stirred those present.
Emotion shook them, they cried, prayed, gesticu-
lated. They did not refuse to go through the activi-
ties dictated by custom; on the contrary. But while
performing them they stripped them of their banal
and customary character. Henceforth these activi-
ties were described as if they had been invented for
the first time, spontaneously, inspired by a passionate sorrow which is unique among sorrows. Certainly the expression of sorrow by survivors is
owing to a new intolerance of separation. But

[5] P. Craven, *Récit d'une soeur* (2 vols.; Paris, 1867).

people were troubled not only at the bedsides of the dying or by the memory of the deceased. The very idea of death moved them.

One of the La Ferronays' granddaughters, a "teenager" of the Romantic era, wrote thoughts of this sort: "Dying is a reward, since it is Heaven. . . . The favorite idea of my entire life [as a child] is death, which has always made me smile. . . . Nothing has ever been able to make the word death lugubrious for me."

An engaged couple in this same family, not yet twenty, were walking in the marvelous gardens of the Villa Pamphili in Rome. "We talked," noted the boy in his secret diary, "for an hour on religion, immortality, and death, which would be sweet, we said, in these beautiful gardens." He added, "I will die young, I have always wanted to." He would be proven right. A few months after his marriage the plague of the century, tuberculosis, carried him off. His wife, a Protestant German, described his last breath: "His eyes, already staring, had turned toward me . . . and I, his wife, I felt what I would never have imagined, *I felt that death was happiness.*" One hesitates to read aloud such a text in America today. How morbid the La Feronnays family must seem!

And yet, were things much different in the America of the 1830s? A contemporary of the little La

Ferronays girl, the fourteen year old Emmeline
Grangerford whom Mark Twain described in
Huckleberry Finn, also lived with the same obses-
sion. She painted "mourning pictures," ladies
weeping over tombs or reading a letter bearing the
sad news. She also kept a secret diary, in which she
copied down the deaths and fatal accidents about
which she read in the *Presbyterian Observer*, and to
this she added the poems which all these misfor-
tunes inspired in her. She was inexhaustible: "She
warn't particular; she could write about anything
you choose to give her to write about just so it was
sadful," observed Mark Twain, laughing behind his
moustache.[6]

One is tempted to explain this overflowing of
macabre affectivity by religion, the emotional religion of romantic Catholicism and of pietism, of
Methodist Protestantism. Religion is certainly a
factor, but the morbid fascination for death is a
sublimation, a religious one it is true, of the erotico-
macabre phantasms of the preceding period.

Thus complaisance toward the idea of death is
the first great change which appears at the end of
the eighteenth century and which has become one
of the characteristics of Romanticism.

---

[6] S. L. Clemens, *The Adventures of Huckleberry Finn* (New York:
Reinhart Editions, 1948), chap. XVII, p. 103.

"Memorial to Washington" (nineteenth-century embroi-
dery and watercolor on silk), from the Eleanor and
Mabel Van Alstyne Folk Art Collection, Smithsonian Institution. Photo from the Smithsonian Institution.

The second great change concerns the relationship between the dying person and his family.

Until the eighteenth century death was a concern for the person threatened by it, and for him alone. Thus it was up to each person to express his ideas, his feelings, his wishes. For that he had available a tool: his last will and testament, which was more than simply a legal document for the disposal of property. From the thirteenth to the eighteenth century the will was the means by which each person could express—often in a very personal manner—his deep thoughts; his religious faith; his attachment to his possessions, to the beings he loved, and to God; and the decisions he had made to assure the salvation of his soul and the repose of his body.

But the purpose of the pious clauses, which sometimes constituted the greatest part of the will, was to involve publicly the executor, the financial directors of the church (*la fabrique*), and the curate of the parish or the monks of the monastery, and to oblige them to carry out the wishes of the deceased.

Indeed, the will, in this form, revealed a distrust of or at least an indifference to the heirs, the close relatives, the family, and the church. By an act deposited with the notary, most often signed by witnesses, the individual making the will imposed his will upon those around him, which means that he was afraid of not otherwise being listened to or obeyed. It was to the same end that he had a stone or metal plaque placed in the church, bearing an excerpt from his will concerning the religious services and the legacy which endowed them. These permanent inscriptions on the walls and pillars of the church were a protection against being forgotten or neglected by both the parish and the family. They had more significance than the grave marker with its "Here lies . . . ."

But in the second half of the eighteenth century, a considerable change occurred in wills. We can assume that this change was common throughout all of the Christian West, both Protestant and Catholic. The pious clauses, the choice of a tomb, the funding of masses and religious services, and the giving of alms all disappeared; the will was reduced to the document we find today, a legal act distributing fortunes. This is a very important event in the history of mentalities, and one to which a French historian, Michel Vovelle, has given the attention it merits.[7]

Thus the will was completely secularized in the eighteenth century. How can we explain this

[7] M. Vovelle, *Piété baroque et déchristianisation* (Paris, 1973). See also, by the same author, "Vision de la mort et au delà en Provence," *Cahiers des Annales*, No. 29 (1970).

phenomenon? It has been thought (and this is Vovelle's thesis) that this secularization was one of the signs of the de-Christianization of society.

I would like to propose another explanation: a distinction was made by the person drawing up the will between his wishes concerning the distribution of his fortune and those wishes inspired by his feelings, his piety, and his affection. The former were still included in the last will and testament. The latter were henceforth expressed orally to those close to him, to the family, spouse, or children. We must not forget the great changes which occurred in the family and which in the eighteenth century ended in new relationships based on feelings and affection. From that time on the sick person on his deathbed would express a confidence in those close to him which had generally been refused them previously. It was no longer necessary to bind them by a legal act.

We are thus at a very important moment in the history of attitudes toward death. In trusting his next of kin, the dying person delegated to them a part of the powers which until then he had jealously exercized. Certainly he still retained the initiative in the ceremonies surrounding his death. He remained, in romantic narratives, the principal and most apparent personage in the activity over which he was presiding, and he would continue to be so until the first three decades of the twentieth century. Even more, as we have just said, romantic complaisance added emphasis to the words and gestures of the dying person. But *the attitude of those present is the most changed.* Though the dying person kept the leading role, the bystanders were no longer the passive, prayerful walk-ons of the past, and, at least from the thirteenth to the eighteenth century, they no longer expressed the great grief of the days of Charlemagne or King Arthur. Indeed, since approximately the twelfth century, the excessive mourning of the High Middle Ages had become ritualized. It only began after death had occurred and it was manifested in the garments and manners and had a specific duration, precisely fixed by custom.

Thus from the end of the Middle Ages to the eighteenth century mourning had a double purpose. On the one hand, it constrained the family of the deceased to demonstrate, at least for a certain period, a sorrow it did not always feel. A hurried remarriage might reduce mourning to a bare minimum, but its observance was never completely eliminated. On the other hand, mourning served to protect the sincerely grieving survivor from the excesses of his grief. It imposed upon him or her a certain type of social life—visits from relatives, neighbors, and friends—which was due him and in the course of which the sorrow might be dissipated without, however, allowing its expression to exceed a level fixed by social conventions. Now, and this is a very important point, in the nineteenth century this level was no longer respected; mourning was unfurled with an uncustomary degree of ostentation. It even claimed to have no obligations to social conventions and to be the most spontaneous and insurmountable expression of a very grave wound: people cried, fainted, languished, and fasted, as the companions of Roland or Launcelot had once done. It was a sort of return to the excessive and spontaneous demonstrations—or apparently spontaneous demonstrations—of the High Middle Ages, after seven centuries of sobriety. The nineteenth century is the era of mourning which the psychologist of today calls *hysterical* mourning. And it is true that at times they almost reached the point of madness, as in the story by Mark Twain, "The Californian's Tale," dated 1893, in which a man who after nineteen years had never accepted his wife's death celebrated the anniversary date of her death by awaiting her impossible return in the company of sympathetic friends who helped him maintain his illusion.

This exaggeration of mourning in the nineteenth century is indeed significant. It means that survivors accepted the death of another person with greater difficulty than in the past. Henceforth, and this is a very important change, the death which is feared is no longer so much the death of the self as the death of another, *la mort de toi*, thy death.

* * *

This feeling lies at the origin of the modern cult of tombs and cemeteries. It is a question of a phenomenon of a religious nature, unique to the contemporary era. Its importance might pass unnoticed by Americans of today, as by the inhabitants of industrial—and Protestant—northwestern Europe, because they would consider it foreign to their culture. An Englishman or an American would not fail to show his repugnance for the baroque excess of the funerary architecture in France or Italy. Yet the phenomenon, though less prevalent, does exist in their cultures. We shall return to this point because it is interesting to see what they have accepted or rejected in a religion of the dead which has been given free rein in Catholic, orthodox Europe.

First let us say that the nineteenth- and twentieth-century cult of tombs has nothing to do with the classical, pre-Christian cults of the dead, nor with any persistence of these observances in folklore. Let us recall what we have already said about the Middle Ages, about the burial *ad sanctos* in churches or against the walls of churches. There was a great chasm between the attitudes of Antiquity concerning the dead and those of the Middle Ages. In the Middle Ages the dead were entrusted to or rather abandoned to the care of the Church, and the exact location of their place of burial was of little importance, most often being indicated neither by a monument nor even by a simple inscription. Certainly by the fourteenth century and especially since the seventeenth century, one can discern a more pronounced concern for marking the site of the tomb, a good indication of a new feeling which was increasingly being expressed, without being able to impose itself completely. The pious or melancholy visit to the tomb of a dear one was an unknown act.

In the second half of the eighteenth century, things changed, and I have been able to study this evolution in France.[8] The accumulation of the dead within the churches or in the small churchyards suddenly became intolerable, at least to the "enlightened" minds of the 1760s. What had been going on for almost a millennium without arousing any scruples became the object of vehement criti-

[8]P. Ariès, "Contribution à l'étude du culte des morts à l'époque contemporaine," *Revue des travaux de l'Académie des Sciences morales et politiques*, Vol. CIX (1966), pp. 25–34.

cism. An entire body of literature bears witness to this. On the one hand, public health was threatened by the pestilential emanations, the unhealthy odors rising from the common graves. On the other hand, the flooring of the churches and the ground of the cemeteries, which were saturated with cadavers, and the exhibition of bones in the charnel houses all constituted a permanent violation of the dignity of the dead. The Church was reproached for having done everything for the soul and nothing for the body, of taking money for masses and showing no concern for the tombs. The example of the Ancients, their piety toward the dead as shown by the remnants of their tombs as at Pompeii and by the eloquence of their funeral inscriptions, was called to mind. The dead should no longer poison the living, and the living should form a veritable lay cult to show their veneration of the dead. Their tombs therefore began to serve as a sign of their presence after death, a presence which did not necessarily derive from the concept of immortality central to religions of salvation such as Christianity. It derived instead from the survivors' unwillingness to accept the departure of their loved one. People held on to the remains. They even went so far as to keep them visible in great bottles of alcohol, as in the case of Necker and his wife, the parents of Madame de Staël. Naturally such ob-

"*Interior of a Church,*" *by Emanuel de Witte, in the Museum Boymans–van Beuningen, Rotterdam.* Photo A. Frequin, Photographie d'Objets d'Art, The Hague.

servances, though they were advocated by certain authors of plans for sepulchers, were not adopted in a general fashion. But the common desire was either to keep the dead at home by burying them on the family property, or else to be able to visit them, if they were buried in a public cemetery. And in order to be able to visit them, the dead had to be "at home," which was not the case in the traditional funeral procedure, in which they were in the church. In the past one was buried before the image of the Virgin or in the chapel of the Holy Sacrament. Now people wanted to go to the very spot where the body had been placed, and they wanted this place to belong totally to the deceased and to his family. It was at this time that the burial concession became a certain form of property, protected from commerce, but assured in perpetuity. This was a very significant innovation. People went to visit the tomb of a dear one as one would go to a relative's home, or into one's own home, full of memories. Memory conferred upon the dead a sort of immortality which was initially foreign to Christianity. From the end of the eighteenth century and even at the height of the nineteenth and twentieth centuries in anticlerical and agnostic France, unbelievers would be the most assiduous visitors to the tombs of their relatives. The visit to the cemetery in France and Italy became, and still is, the great continuing religious act. Those who no longer go to church still go to the cemetery, where they have become accustomed to place flowers on the tombs. They meditate there, that is to say they evoke the dead person and cultivate his memory.

Thus it is a private cult, but also from its very origins, a public one. The cult of memory immediately spread from the individual to society as a result of one and the same wave of sensibility. The eighteenth-century authors of cemetery plans wanted cemeteries to serve both as parks organized for family visits and as museums for illustrious persons, like St. Paul's Cathedral in London.[9] There the tombs of heroes and great men would be venerated by the State. This was a different conception from that of the dynastic chapels or crypts such as Saint-Denis, Westminster, the Escorial, or the Capuchins of Vienna.

A new concept of society was born at the end of the eighteenth century; it developed during the nineteenth century and found its expression in Auguste Comte's positivism, an intellectualized form of nationalism. It was thought, and even felt,

[9] Plans submitted to the procureur général of the Parlement of Paris in accordance with the royal decree of 1776 closing the old cemeteries and ordering their transfer outside the city, papers of Joly de Fleury, Bibliothèque nationale, ms. fr. 1209, folios 62–87.

that society is composed of both the dead and the living. The city of the dead is the obverse of the society of the living, or rather than the obverse, it is its image, its intemporal image. For the dead have gone through the moment of change, and their monuments are the visible sign of the permanence of their city.

Thus the cemetery once again gained a place in the city—a place both physical and moral—which it had lost in the early Middle Ages, but which it had occupied throughout Antiquity. What would we know about ancient civilization without the objects, the inscriptions, and the iconography found by archeologists while excavating tombs? Our tombs are empty, but much can be learned from our cemeteries, the size of which speaks eloquently about our mentality. Indeed, the piety and the new respect shown for tombs resulted in an extension of the surface area of cemeteries, because it had become intolerable and forbidden to pile up corpses as in the charnel houses of the Middle Ages. Thus the place reserved for the dead became increasingly intrusive, which soon aroused concern among the authorities. But public opinion resisted attempts to end the propagation of cemeteries.

During Napoleon III's reign, the administration wanted to deconsecrate the Parisian cemeteries,

which had in the early nineteenth century been
planned outside the city but which had been
enveloped by urban expansion. They could evoke a
precedent for this: at the end of Louis XVI's reign
the old Cemetery of the Innocents, which had been
in use for more than five centuries, had been razed,
plowed, dug up, and built over, to the great indifference of the population. But in the second half
of the nineteenth century the mentality had
changed. Public opinion rose against the govern-
ment's sacrilegious projects, a unanimous public
opinion in which the Catholics united with their
positivist enemies. Henceforth the cemetery appeared a necessary part of the city. Today the cult
of the dead is one of the forms or expressions of
patriotism. Thus in France the anniversary of the
victorious conclusion of World War I is considered
the feast-day of dead soldiers. It is celebrated at
the Monument to the Dead, to be found in every
French village, no matter how small. Without a
monument to the dead the victory could not be
celebrated. In the new cities created by recent industrial development, the absence of a monument
to the dead thus created a quandry. The problem
was solved by virtually annexing the monument of
a nearby, deserted little village.[10] For this monu-

[10]This is what occurred at Lacq, near Pau, where the exploiting of
natural gas resulted in the creation of a new industrial city.

ment is indeed a tomb, an empty one of course, but it perpetuates memory, a *monumentum.*

* * *

We now reach a point in this long evolution at which we should pause and introduce a new factor. We have followed variations in time, a long but still changing time. We have scarcely, except for a few details, considered variations in locations. We might say that the phenomena which we are studying here were approximately the same through all of Western civilization. But, in the course of the nineteenth century this similarity in mentalities changed and important differences appeared. We see North America, England, and a part of northwestern Europe break away from France, Germany, and Italy. What does this differentiation involve, and what is its meaning?

In the nineteenth century and until World War I (a great revolution in mores) the difference was scarcely apparent either in the protocol of funerals or in mourning customs. But this difference can be observed in cemeteries and in the art on tombstones. Our English friends do not fail to point out to us continentals how extravagantly baroque our cemeteries are—take the Campo Santo of Genoa or the old (nineteenth-century) cemeteries of our major French cities with their tombs surmounted by statues writhing, embracing one another, and lamenting. There is no doubt that at that time a great transformation occurred.

At the end of the eighteenth century, cemeteries were similar throughout the Western world; in England, North America, and parts of northwestern Europe the same model persists today. The English cemetery of today closely resembles what the French cemetery had been until the end of the eighteenth century, when burial in churches and even within the city limits was forbidden. We find it intact in America, for example in Alexandria, Virginia: a bit of countryside and nature, a pretty English garden in a setting of grass, moss, and trees, sometimes but not necessarily still adjacent to the church.

The tombs of this period were a combination of the two elements which until then had generally been used separately: the horizontal flat tombstone, and the "Here-lies" type of stone establishing a bequest, a stone which was vertical because it was to be affixed to a wall. In France, in the few late-eighteenth-century cemeteries that are still extant, the two elements are juxtaposed. In colonial America the vertical element was generally the only one kept. A stone stele was erected at the head of the grave, which was itself merely covered with grass, while the foot was occasionally indicated by a small marker. In both cases the inscription was placed on the vertical headstone. The inscription, both biographic and elegiac, was the only luxury of these sepulchers, which made a show of simplicity. This simplicity was only disregarded in cases of famous persons whose destiny had provided an example for the national necropolis, or dramatic or extraordinary deaths. This cemetery was the end product of a search for simplicity which can be followed in its different forms throughout all of Western civilization, in the second half of the eighteenth and throughout the nineteenth century, even in papal Rome, where baroque customs persist.

This simplicity did not imply a disloyalty to the loved one; to the contrary. It fitted in very well with the melancholy of the romantic cult of the dead. This cult found its first poet in England: Thomas Gray, author of "Elegy in a Country Churchyard." The Elegy! It was translated into French, one particular version being by André Chénier, and it served as a model for others.

It is in America, in Washington, D.C., even more than in the Panthéon of Paris, that we find the first major manifestations of the funeral cult of the hero. In a city filled with commemorative monuments, such as those to Washington, Jefferson, and Lincoln—which are "tombs" without sepulchers—a twentieth-century European encounters an even stranger phenomenon: Arlington Cemetery. Here, despite its public and national character, the garden of the Lee-Custis House has preserved its appearance of a private estate.

Although astonishing to a European of today, the civic and funerary landscape at Arlington and along the Mall sprang from the same sentiment that caused a multiplicity of monuments to the war dead in the France of the 1920s, monuments which are doubtlessly today quite incomprehensible to the descendents of those who created Arlington and the center of Washington.

Thus, regardless of religious differences, simplicity and the romantic, hero cults formed the common denominator throughout Western civilization in the late eighteenth and early nineteenth centuries. And it is here that we find the point of departure. The United States and northwestern Europe were to remain more or less faithful to this old model, while continental Europe strayed away and constructed for its dead monuments which became increasingly complicated and figurative.

A careful study of an American custom would perhaps help us find an explanation for this:

"mourning pictures." These lithographs or em-
broidered panels, now found in museums, were in-
tended to decorate the home. They played the role
of the tomb, of the memorial, a sort of portable
tomb adapted to American mobility—if this mobility is not at that time an anachronistic myth. Likewise, in the museum of York, England, we find
Victorian funeral announcements which are repro-
ductions of neo-gothic funeral chapels, those very
chapels which served as models for the French
tomb builders of the same period. It is as if the
English and the Americans of the day were committing to paper or silk—ephemeral substances—
what the continental Europeans were portraying
on tombstones.

One is obviously tempted to attribute this difference to the contrast between Protestantism and
Catholicism. This explanation appears suspect to
the historian, at least at first glance. Indeed, the
separation of the churches by the Council of Trent
occurred much earlier than this divorce in funeral
attitudes. Throughout the seventeenth century
people were buried in exactly the same fashion
(with variations in the liturgy, of course) in Pepys'
England, in the Holland of those genre painters
who specialized in church interiors, and in French
and Italian churches. The mental attitudes were the
same.

Yet there appears to be some truth in the religious explanation when we realize that during the nineteenth century Catholicism developed sentimental, emotional means of expression which it had avoided in the eighteenth century, after the great baroque rhetoric: a sort of romantic neo-baroquism. That type of Catholicism, especially in France, became a quite different thing from that of the seventeenth and eighteenth centuries.

Nevertheless, we must not forget what we were saying a short time ago: that the exalted and emotive nature of the cult of the dead did not have a Christian origin. It had a positivist origin, and the Catholics rallied to it and assimilated it so perfectly that they thought it indigenous to their religion.

Should we not instead implicate the nature of the socio-economic revolution of the nineteenth century? More than religion, the rate of industrialization and urbanization intervened. Neo-baroque funeral attitudes developed in cultures in which, even in towns and large cities, economic growth was less rapid and rural influences persisted. I have put the question before you. I think it should be an interesting one for the historians of American mentalities.

In any case, a fault line became evident, and the crack would widen toward the middle of the twentieth century. The great twentieth-century re-

WESTERN ATTITUDES TOWARD DEATH

fusal to accept death is incomprehensible if we do not take this fault line into account, for this refusal was born and developed on only one side of that frontier.

Forbidden Death

Duringthelongperiodwehavecovered, from the High Middle Ages until the mid-nineteenth century, the attitude toward death changed, but so slowly that contemporaries did not even notice. In our day, in approximately a third of a century, we have witnessed a brutal revolution in traditional ideas and feelings, a revolution so brutal that social observers have not failed to be struck by it. It is really an absolutely unheard-of phenomenon. Death, so omnipresent in the past that it was familiar, would be effaced, would disappear. It would become shameful and forbidden.[1]

[1]P. Ariès, "La mort inversée," *Archives européennes de sociologie*, Vol. VIII (1967), pp. 169-95.

This revolution occurred in a well defined cultural area, where in the nineteenth century the cult of the dead and of cemeteries did not experience the great development noted in France, Italy, and Spain. It even seems that this revolution began in the United States and spread to England, to the Netherlands, to industrialized Europe; and we can see it today, before our very eyes, reaching France and leaving oil smudges wherever the wave passes.

At its beginning doubtlessly lies a sentiment already expressed during the second half of the nineteenth century: those surrounding the dying person had a tendency to spare him and to hide from him the gravity of his condition. Yet they admitted that this dissimulation could not last too long, except in such extraordinary cases as those described by Mark Twain in 1902 in "Was it Heaven or Hell?" The dying person must one day know, but the relatives no longer had the cruel courage to tell the truth themselves.

In short, at this point the truth was beginning to be challenged.

The first motivation for the lie was the desire to spare the sick person, to assume the burden of his ordeal. But this sentiment, whose origin we know (the intolerance of another's death and the confidence shown by the dying person in those about him) very rapidly was covered over by a different sentiment, a new sentiment characteristic of modernity: one must avoid—no longer for the sake of the dying person, but for society's sake, for the sake of those close to the dying person—the disturbance and the overly strong and unbearable emotion caused by the ugliness of dying and by the very presence of death in the midst of a happy life, for it is henceforth given that life is always happy or should always seem to be so. Nothing had yet changed in the rituals of death, which were preserved at least in appearance, and no one had yet had the idea of changing them. But people had already begun to empty them of their dramatic impact; the procedure of hushing-up had begun. This is very noticeable in Tolstoy's stories about death.

Between 1930 and 1950 the evolution accelerated markedly. This was due to an important physical phenomenon: the displacement of the site of death. One no longer died at home in the bosom of one's family, but in the hospital, alone.

One dies in the hospital because the hospital has become the place to receive care which can no longer be given at home. Previously the hospital had been a shelter for the poor, for pilgrims; then it became a medical center where people were healed, where one struggled against death. It still has that curative function, but people are also beginning to consider a certain type of hospital as the designated spot for dying. One dies in the hospital because the doctor did not succeed in healing. One no longer goes to or will go to the hospital to be healed, but for the specific purpose of dying. American sociologists have observed that there are today two types of seriously ill persons to be found in hospitals.[2] The most archaic are recent immigrants who are still attached to the traditions of death, who try to snatch the dying person from the hospital so he can die at home, *more majorum*; the others are those more involved in modernity who come to die in the hospital because it has become inconvenient to die at home.

Death in the hospital is no longer the occasion of a ritual ceremony, over which the dying person presides amidst his assembled relatives and friends. Death is a technical phenomenon obtained by a cessation of care, a cessation determined in a more or less avowed way by a decision of the doctor and the hospital team. Indeed, in the majority of cases the dying person has already lost consciousness. Death has been dissected, cut to bits by a series of little steps, which finally makes it impossible to know which step was the real death, the one in

[2] B. G. Glasser and A. L. Strauss, *Awareness of Dying* (Chicago, 1965).

which consciousness was lost, or the one in which breathing stopped. All these little silent deaths have replaced and erased the great dramatic act of death, and no one any longer has the strength or patience to wait over a period of weeks for a moment which has lost a part of its meaning.

From the end of the eighteenth century we had been impressed by a sentimental landslide which was causing the initiative to pass from the dying man himself to his family—a family in which henceforth he would have complete confidence. Today the initiative has passed from the family, as much an outsider as the dying person, to the doctor and the hospital team. They are the masters of death—of the moment as well as of the circumstances of death—and it has been observed that they try to obtain from their patient "an acceptable style of living while dying." The accent has been placed on "acceptable." An acceptable death is a death which can be accepted or tolerated by the survivors. It has its antithesis: "the embarrassingly graceless dying," which embarrasses the survivors because it causes too strong an emotion to burst forth; and emotions must be avoided both in the hospital and everywhere in society. One does not have the right to become emotional other than in private, that is to say, secretly. Here, then, is what has happened to the great death scene, which had changed so little over the centuries, if not the millennia.

The funeral rites have also been modified. Let us put aside for a moment the American case. In England and northwestern Europe, they are trying to reduce to a decent minimum the inevitable operations necessary to dispose of the body. It is above all essential that society—the neighbors, friends, colleagues, and children—notice to the least possible degree that death has occurred. If a few formalities are maintained, and if a ceremony still marks the departure, it must remain discreet and must avoid emotion. Thus the family reception line for receiving condolences at the end of the funeral service has now been suppressed. The outward manifestations of mourning are repugned and are disappearing. Dark clothes are no longer worn; one no longer dresses differently than on any other day.

Too evident sorrow does not inspire pity but repugnance, it is the sign of mental instability or of bad manners: it is *morbid.* Within the family circle one also hesitates to let himself go for fear of upsetting the children. One only has the right to cry if no one else can see or hear. Solitary and shameful mourning is the only recourse, like a sort of masturbation. (The comparison is Gorer's.)

In countries in which the death revolution has
been radical, once the dead person has been evacu-
ated, his tomb is no longer visited. In England for
example, cremation has become the dominant
manner of burial. When cremation occurs, sometimes with dispersal of the ashes, the cause is more
than a desire to break with Christian tradition; it is
a manifestation of enlightenment, of modernity.
The deep motivation is that cremation is the most
radical means of getting rid of the body and of
forgetting it, of nullifying it, of being "too final."
Despite the efforts of cemetery offices, people
rarely visit the urns today, though they may still
visit gravesides. Cremation excludes a pilgrimage.

We would be committing an error if we entirely
attributed this flight from death to an indifference
toward the dead person. In reality the contrary is
true. In the old society, the panoply of mourning
scarcely concealed a rapid resignation. How many
widowers remarried a few short months after the
death of their wives! On the contrary, today,
where mourning is forbidden, it has been noted
that the mortality rate of widows or widowers during the year following the spouse's death is much
higher than that of the control group of the same
age.

The point has even been reached at which, according to Gorer's observations, the choking back

of sorrow, the forbidding of its public manifestation, the obligation to suffer alone and secretly,
has aggravated the trauma stemming from the loss
of a dear one. In a family in which sentiment is
given an important place and in which premature
death is becoming increasingly rare (save in the
event of an automobile accident), the death of a
near relative is always deeply felt, as it was in the
Romantic era.

A single person is missing for you, and the whole
world is empty. But one no longer has the right to
say so aloud.

* * *

The combination of phenomena which we have
just analyzed is nothing other than the imposition
of an interdict. What was once required is henceforth forbidden.

The merit of having been the first to define this
unwritten law of our civilization goes to the English sociologist, Geoffrey Gorer.[3] He has shown
clearly how death has become a taboo and how in
the twentieth century it has replaced sex as the
principal forbidden subject. Formerly children
were told that they were brought by the stork, but
they were admitted to the great farewell scene

[3] G. Gorer, *Death, Grief, and Mourning in Contemporary Britain*
(New York, 1965), a key work.

about the bed of the dying person. Today they are initiated in their early years to the physiology of love; but when they no longer see their grandfather and express astonishment, they are told that he is resting in a beautiful garden among the flowers. Such is "The Pornography of Death"—the title of a pioneering article by Gorer, published in 1955— and the more society was liberated from the Victorian constraints concerning sex, the more it rejected things having to do with death. Along with the interdict appears the transgression: the mixture of eroticism and death so sought after from the sixteenth to the eighteenth century reappears in our sadistic literature and in violent death in our daily life.

This establishment of an interdict has profound meaning. It is already difficult to isolate the meaning of the interdict on sex which was precipitated by the Christian confusion between sin and sexuality (though, as in the nineteenth century, this interdict was never imposed). But the interdict on death suddenly follows upon the heels of a very long period—several centuries—in which death was a public spectacle from which no one would have thought of hiding and which was even sought after at times.

The cause of the interdict is at once apparent: the need for happiness—the moral duty and the social obligation to contribute to the collective happiness by avoiding any cause for sadness or boredom, by appearing to be always happy, even if in the depths of despair. By showing the least sign of sadness, one sins against happiness, threatens it, and society then risks losing its *raison d'être*.

In a book addressed to Americans which appeared in 1958, Jacques Maritain evoked the inalterable optimism of the dentists in an American small town.[4] "You reach the point of thinking in a sort of dream that the act of dying amid happy smiles, amid white garments like angels' wings, would be a veritable pleasure, a moment of no consequence. Relax, take it easy, it's nothing."

The idea of happiness brings us back to the United States, and it is now appropriate to attempt to understand the relationships between American civilization and the modern attitude toward death.

* * *

It seems that the modern attitude toward death, that is to say the interdiction of death in order to preserve happiness, was born in the United States around the beginning of the twentieth century. However, on its native soil the interdict was not

[4] J. Maritain, *Reflections on America* (New York, 1965), p. 91.

carried to its ultimate extremes. In American society it encountered a braking influence which it did not encounter in Europe. Thus the American attitude toward death today appears as a strange compromise between trends which are pulling it in two nearly opposite directions.

There is as yet very scanty documentation on this subject, but the little that is available has inspired the following thoughts, which I hope will evoke comments, corrections, and criticism from American historians.

When I read for the first time G. Gorer, J. Mitford, H. Feifel, etc.,[5] I thought I was finding in contemporary America traces of the mentality of the French Enlightenment.

"Forest Lawn" is not as futuristic as Evelyn Waugh thought,[6] and it made me think of the descriptions of the cemeteries dreamed of by the French authors of cemetery plans in the late eighteenth century, plans which never materialized owing to the Revolution and which were replaced in the early nineteenth century by the more declamatory and figurative architecture of Romanticism. In the United States, everything was happen-

---

[5] J. Mitford, *The American Way of Death* (New York, 1963); H. Feifel *et al.*, *The Meaning of Death* (New York, 1959), a pioneering work.

[6] E. Waugh, *The Loved One* (London, 1948).

ing as if the Romantic interval had never existed, and as if the mentality of the eighteenth-century Enlightenment had persisted without interruption.

This first impression, this first hypothesis, was false. It did not take sufficient account of American Puritanism, which is incompatible with confidence in man, in his goodness, in his happiness. Excellent American historians pointed this out to me, and I was very willing to agree with them. Yet the similarities between a part of the current American attitude toward death and that of enlightened Europe in the eighteenth century are no less troubling. We must concede that the mental phenomena which we have just observed occur much later than the French Enlightenment. In America, during the eighteenth and the first half of the nineteenth centuries, and even later, burials conformed to tradition, especially in the countryside: the carpenter made the coffin (the coffin, not yet the "casket"); the family and friends saw to its transport and to the procession itself; and the pastor and gravedigger carried out the service. In the early nineteenth century the grave was still sometimes dug on the family property—which is a modern act, copied from the Ancients, and which was unknown in Europe before the mid-eighteenth century and with few exceptions was rapidly abandoned. In villages and small towns the cemetery most frequently lay adjacent to the church. In the cities, once again paralleling Europe, the cemetery had in about 1830 been situated outside the city but was encompassed by urban growth and abandoned toward 1870 for a new site. It soon fell into ruin and Mark Twain tells us how the skeletons would leave it at night, carrying off with them what remained of their tombs ("A Curious Dream," 1870).

The old cemeteries were church property, as they had been in Europe and still are in England. The new cemeteries belonged to private associations, as the French authors of those eighteenth-century plans had fruitlessly dreamed. In Europe cemeteries became municipal, that is to say public, property and were never left to private initiative.

In the growing cities of the nineteenth century, old carpenters or gravediggers, or owners of carts and horses, became "undertakers," and the manipulation of the dead became a profession. Here history is still completely comparable to that in Europe, at least in that part of Europe which remained faithful to the eighteenth-century canons of simplicity and which remained outside the pale of Romantic bombast.

Things seem to have changed during the period of the Civil War. Today's "morticians," whose letters-patent go back to that period, give as their ancestor a quack doctor expelled from the school of medicine, Dr. Holmes, who had a passion for dissection and cadavers. He would offer his services to the victim's family and embalmed, it is said, 4,000 cadavers unaided in four years. That's not a bad rate for the period! Why such recourse to embalming? Had it been practiced previously? Is there an American tradition going back to the eighteenth century, a period in which throughout Europe there was a craze for embalming? Yet this technique was abandoned in nineteenth-century Europe, and the wars did not resurrect it. It is noteworthy that embalming became a career in the United States before the end of the century, even if it was not yet very widespread. We can cite the case of Elizabeth "Ma" Green, born in 1884, who as a young woman began to help the undertaker in her small town. At the age of twenty she was a "licensed embalmer" and made a career of this trade until her death. In 1900 embalming appeared in California. We know that it has today become a very widespread method of preparing the dead, a practice almost unknown in Europe and characteristic of the American way of death.

One cannot help thinking that this long-accepted and avowed preference for embalming has a meaning, even if it is difficult to interpret.

This meaning could indeed be that of a certain refusal to accept death, either as a familiar end to which one is resigned, or as a dramatic sign in the Romantic manner. And this meaning became even more obvious when death became an object of commerce and of profit. It is not easy to sell something which has no value because it is too familiar and common, or something which is frightening, horrible, or painful. In order to sell death, it had to be made friendly. But we may assume that "funeral directors"—since 1885 a new name for undertakers—would not have met with success if public opinion had not cooperated. They presented themselves not as simple sellers of services, but as "doctors of grief" who have a mission, as do doctors and priests; and this mission, from the beginning of this century, consists in aiding the mourning survivors to return to normalcy. The new funeral director ("new" because he has replaced the simple undertaker) is a "doctor of grief," an "expert at returning abnormal minds to normal in the shortest possible time." They are "members of an exalted, almost sacred calling."[7]

Thus mourning is no longer a necessary period imposed by society; it has become a *morbid state*

[7] From Mitford, *The American Way of Death*.

which must be treated, shortened, erased by the "doctor of grief."

Through a series of little steps we can see the birth and development of the ideas which would end in the present-day interdict, built upon the ruins of Puritanism, in an urbanized culture which is dominated by rapid economic growth and by the search for happiness linked to the search for profit.

This process should normally result in the situation of England today, as it is described, for example, by Gorer: the almost total suppression of everything reminding us of death.

But, and this is what is unique about the American attitude, American mores have not gone to such an extreme; they stopped along the way. Americans are very willing to transform death, to put make-up on it, to sublimate it, but they do not want to make it disappear. Obviously, this would also mark the end of profit, but the money earned by funeral merchants would not be tolerated if they did not meet a profound need. The wake, increasingly avoided in industrial Europe, persists in the United States: it exists as "viewing the remains," the "visitation." "They don't *view* bodies in England."[8]

[8]*Ibid.*

The visit to the cemetery and a certain veneration in regard to the tomb also persist. That is why public opinion—and funeral directors—finds cremation distasteful, for it gets rid of the remains too quickly and too radically.

Burials are not shameful and they are not hidden. With that very characteristic mixture of commerce and idealism, they are the object of showy publicity, like any other consumer's item, be it soap or religion. Seen for example in the buses of New York City in 1965 was the following ad, purchased by one of the city's leading morticians: "The dignity and integrity of a Gawler. Funeral costs no more. . . . Easy access, private parking for over 100 cars." Such publicity would be unthinkable in Europe, first of all because it would repel the customer rather than attract him.

Thus we must admit that a traditional resistance has kept alive certain rituals of death which had been abandoned or are being abandoned in industrialized Europe, especially among the middle classes.

Nevertheless, though these rituals have been continued, they have also been transformed. The American way of death is the synthesis of two tendencies: one traditional, the other euphoric.

Thus during the wakes or farewell "visitations" which have been preserved, the visitors come without shame or repugnance. This is because in reality they are not visiting a dead person, as they traditionally have, but an almost-living one who, thanks to embalming, is still present, as if he were awaiting you to greet you or to take you off on a walk. The definitive nature of the rupture has been blurred. Sadness and mourning have been banished from this calming reunion.

Perhaps because American society has not totally accepted the interdict, it can more easily challenge it; but this interdict is spreading in the Old World, where the cult of the dead would seem more deeply rooted.

During the last ten years in American publications an increasing number of sociologists and psychologists have been studying the conditions of death in contemporary society and especially in hospitals.[9] This bibliography makes no mention of the current conditions of funerals and mourning. They are deemed satisfactory. On the other hand, the authors have been struck by the manner of dying, by the inhumanity, the cruelty of solitary death in hospitals and in a society where death has lost the prominent place which custom had granted

---

[9] A bibliography of 340 recent works is to be found in O. G. Brim *et al., The Dying Patient* (New York: Russell Sage Foundation, 1970). It does not include anything having to do with funerals, cemeteries, mourning, or suicide.

it over the millennia, a society where the interdiction of death paralyzes and inhibits the reactions of the medical staff and family involved. These publications are also preoccupied with the fact that death has become the object of a voluntary decision by the doctors and the family, a decision which today is made shamefacedly, clandestinely. And this para-medical literature, for which, as far as I know, there is no equivalent in Europe, is bringing death back into the dialogue from which it had been excluded. Death is once again becoming something one can talk about. Thus the interdict is threatened, but only in the place where it was born and where it encountered limitations. Elsewhere, in the other industrialized societies, it is maintaining or extending its empire.

* * *

CONCLUSION

Now let us try, as a sort of conclusion, to understand the general meaning of the changes which we have discerned and analyzed.

First of all, we encountered a very old, very durable, very massive sentiment of familiarity with death, with neither fear nor despair, half-way between passive resignation and mystical trust.

Even more than during the other vigorous periods of existence, Destiny was revealed through death, and in those days the dying person accepted it in a public ceremony whose ritual was fixed by custom. The ceremony of death was then at least as important as the ceremony of the funeral and mourning. Death was the awareness by each person of a *Destiny* in which his own personality was not annihilated but *put to sleep—requies, dormitio*. This *requies* presupposed a survivial, though a deadened and weakened one, the grey survival of the shades or *larvae* of paganism, of the ghosts of old and popular Christianity. This belief did not make as great a distinction as we today make between the time before and the time after, the life and the afterlife. The living and the dead in both medieval literature and in popular folk tales show the same simple and vague, yet rather racy natures. On both sides of death, one is still very near the deep wellsprings of sentiment.

This way of dying signified a surrender of the self to Destiny and an indifference to the too-individual and diverse forms of the personality. It lasted as long as familiarity with death and with the dead lasted, at least until the Romantic era.

But from the Middle Ages on, among the litterati, in the upper classes, it was subtly modified, while retaining its traditional characteristics.

Death ceased being the forgetting of a self which was vigorous but without ambition; it ceased being the acceptance of an overwhelming Destiny, but one which concealed no novelty. Instead it became a place where the individual traits of each life, of each biography, appeared in the bright light of the clear conscience, a place where everything was weighed, counted, written down, where everything could be changed, lost, or saved. In this second Middle Ages, from the thirteenth to the fifteenth century, in which were laid the bases of what was to become modern civilization, a more personal, more inner feeling about death, about the death of the self, betrayed the violent attachment to the things of life but likewise—and this is the meaning of the macabre iconography of the fourteenth century—it betrayed the bitter feeling of failure, mingled with mortality: *a passion for being, an anxiety at not sufficiently being.*

In the modern period, death, despite the apparent continuity of themes and ritual, became challenged and was furtively pushed out of the world of familiar things. In the realm of the imagination it became allied with eroticism in order to express the break with the established order. In religion it signified, more than it had in the Middle Ages—which, however, gave birth to this way of thinking—a scorn for the world and an image of the void. In the family—even when they believed in the afterlife, and in a more realistic afterlife, a transposition of life into eternity—death became the unaccepted separation, the death of the other, "thy death," the death of the loved one.

Thus death gradually assumed another form, both more distant and more dramatic, more full of tension. Death was sometimes exalted (the beautiful death in Lamartine) and soon was impugned (the ugly death of Madame Bovary).

In the nineteenth century death appeared omnipresent: funeral processions, mourning clothes, the spread of cemeteries and of their surface area, visits and pilgrimages to tombs, the cult of memory. But did this pomp not hide the weakening of old familiarities, which alone were really deeply rooted? In any case, this eloquent decor of death toppled in our day, and death has become *unnamable*. Everything henceforth goes on as if neither I nor those who are dear to me are any longer mortal. Technically, we admit that we might die; we take out insurance on our lives to protect our families from poverty. But really, at heart we feel we are nonmortals. And surprise! Our life is not as a result gladdened!

Is there a permanent relationship between one's idea of death and one's idea of oneself? If this is the case, must we take for granted, on the one hand, contemporary man's recoil from the desire to exist, the inverse of what occurred during the second Middle Ages, the thirteenth to fifteenth centuries? And, on the other hand, must we take for granted that it is impossible for our technological cultures ever to regain the naive confidence in Destiny which had for so long been shown by simple men when dying?

Index

INDEX

This book was composed in Aldine Roman text and Garamond
display by Jones Composition Company, Inc. from a
design by Victoria Dudley. It was printed on Maple's Danforth
stock and bound in Columbia Bayside cloth by
The Maple Press Company.

Library of Congress Cataloging in Publication Data

Ariès, Philippe.
    Western attitudes toward death.

    (Johns Hopkins symposia in comparative history) Includes
    bibliographical references.
    1. Death—Collected works. I. Title. II. Series.
BD444.A6713   128'.5   73-19340
ISBN 0-8018-1566-5